Carole writes from the heart of a catechist dir
catechist. I highly recommend that parish cate⌇⌇⌇⌇ ⌇⌇⌇ ⌇⌇⌇ ⌇
book together.

■ **MARY JO WAGGONER, DIRECTOR**
Office for Evangelization and Catechetical Ministry, Diocese of San Diego

---

Realistic yet filled with the ideal, light-hearted but profound, creative as
well as doable, *Catechist 101: Wade Don't Dive* is rooted in deep reverence
for the call of each catechist and insightful respect for every learner.

■ **JANET SCHAEFFLER, OP,** *Author, Retreat and Catechetical Presenter*

Where was this book when I started? Carole has something for everyone
wading in the water of catechetical ministry.

■ **DIANE BLAIR, MAPS,** *Loyola Institute for Ministry Admissions and
Student Services, Loyola University New Orleans*

Carole Eipers, one of the nation's leading "faith storytellers," offers
here an accessible and common-sense resource that new and seasoned
catechists cannot afford to be without.

■ **GERARD F. BAUMBACH** *Emeritus Professor, Institute for Church Life
Director Emeritus of the Echo Program, University of Notre Dame*

This is a book to be read at the beginning of every catechetical year.
It provides inspiration, enthusiasm, and valuable ideas to enhance our
teaching. Our students deserve it. ■ **SISTER ROSA MONIQUE PENA, OP**
Bilingual Catechetical Consultant, William H Sadlier Inc.

Catechist 101 captures the essence of answering the call to be a catechist.
This is a great resource that every catechist young and old would benefit
from by reading and re-reading. ■ **DAN McGOWAN,** *Director of Faith Formation
Resurrection Catholic Church and School, Lakeland, FL*

Carole provides practical advice and inspiring illustrations to assist
catechists to swim with confidence. I would invite both new and veteran
catechists to lift the cover and dive in! ■ **THOMAS P. WALTERS, PHD,**
*Emeritus Professor of Religious Education, Saint Meinrad Seminary
and School of Theology*

Catechist 101 is filled with a variety of practical suggestions and the hope-
filled encouragement needed to empower every catechist.

■ **MARGE GARBACZ** *Pastoral Associate/Director of Religious Education
St. Symphorosa Parish, Chicago, IL*

Carole addresses the fears and questions of both new and experienced catechists in an affirming and gentle way. She makes catechesis doable.
▓ **DON KURRE,** *Director of Religious Education Diocese of Grand Island, Nebraska*

Carole weaves storytelling with practical tools to help new and seasoned catechists critically reflect on the great job they are doing.
▓ **JOSÉ M. AMAYA**
Director of Faith Formation, Archdiocese for the Military Services, USA

I love this book. I want to give it to all my catechists. For pastors and DREs who are looking for something that will help form and support the ministry of catechists—this is it!" ▓ **FR. RON LEWINSKI,** *Pastor St. Mary of the Annuciation Parish, Mundelein, Illinois*

Carole's ideas and suggestions are clear, fresh, and sparkling. This book should be requirement for anyone preparing to be a catechist in a diocesan training program as well as for the seasoned catechist.
▓ **FATHER MICHAEL CARRANO,** *Pastor Our Lady of Hope Parish, Middle Village, Queens New York*

Dr. Eipers uses a gentle approach, filled with stories and analogies to share her experience and wisdom. I highly recommend this book for all catechists and Catholic school teachers. ▓ **ROBERT PRAZNIK,** *Superintendent, Archdiocese of Winnipeg Catholic Schools*

Carole's analogies are right on target and speak to the heart and soul of catechetical ministry. I am going to give it to my current catechists and to those I am hoping will join our program as catechists!
▓ **TERRY NAVARRO**
Pastoral Assoc./Dir. of Religious Ed , St. Mary Star of the Sea Parish

Carole has artfully woven practical advice with her own witness of faith. Both new and experienced catechists can benefit.
▓ **LORI DAHLHOFF, EDD,** *Executive Director, NCEA Religious Education Department*

Carole Eipers gives us the confidence and skill to share God with those who come to us in trust and love. Enjoy the water!
▓ **FATHER TERRY JOHNSON,** *Pastor, St. Irenaeus Parish, Park Forest Illinois*

The ESSENTIAL CATECHIST'S BOOKSHELF

Catechist
101

WADE DON'T DIVE

GIVING NEW *and*
SEASONED CATECHISTS
CONFIDENCE

Carole M. Eipers, D.Min.

Dedication

To Nicholas Robert
and those who taught me to "swim"
and keep me afloat.

Second Printing 2014

Twenty-Third Publications
1 Montauk Avenue, Suite 200, New London, CT 06320
(860) 437-3012 » (800) 321-0411 » www.23rdpublications.com

ISBN: 978-1-58595-948-8
Library of Congress Catalog Card Number: 2013957104
Printed in the U.S.A.

Contents

Introduction *1*

1 C'mon in! The water's fine! *3*

2 But I can't swim! *11*

3 Stick your toe in. *19*

4 Stay close to shore *27*

5 Never swim alone (and you never do) *35*

6 Wanna go deeper?. *43*

7 Paddle and kick *51*

8 Staying afloat. *59*

9 Life savers. *67*

10 Life preservers. *75*

11 Now dive! *83*

An INTRODUCTION *and* INVITATION

Dear Catechist,

The word game called *Mad Libs* has been around since 1953, and in its latest morphing is into an app for smartphones. As I wrote this book for you and other catechists, I wondered what you would be thinking and feeling as you read the chapters.

Mad Libs came to mind. I thought if I wrote a story in which some of the words were missing and you could fill in the blanks, it could capture where you are at this moment in your catechetical ministry journey. So, I invite you to fill in the blanks, to tell your story as you begin this book. There will be another story—or rather, a continuation of your story—for you to complete as you finish this book.

I wrote this book while I was at the beach and so the images of learning to swim were in my mind as I thought about your beginning to be a catechist—or beginning again. Don't rush it! You don't have to "cover it all" or "finish the book" all at once. Enjoy the lessons and then the children will enjoy learning their faith and will continue to come and to learn.

So, let's wade in!

Blessings,

Carole

My Story

THE _____ CATECHIST

It is now "once upon a time" and it seems it's time to
_____. "_____!" I find myself ex-
claiming when I think about being a catechist. I am feeling _____ and _____ as I consider
this responsibility. The one thing that I know is that I am

_____.

The children I will be teaching are _____ years
old and they are all _____. I worry that they might

_____.

My own faith is _____. Sharing my faith makes
me wonder if I am _____. After all, there are others
who could be catechists but they _____.

What I need now is to _____. And I
need to learn about _____. I hope that I
will be _____ and that my students will be

_____.

And so I pray:

Dear _____,

I thank you for _____. I am _____ as
I prepare to be a catechist. Please give me _____ and
_____ and _____.

Help me to remember that I am _____ and that
as long as I have _____, I can do this ministry for you.

Amen.

C'mon in!
The water's fine!

"No."

When I was first asked to be a catechist, that was my immediate response. First of all, I was not even sure what a catechist was. Second, whatever it was, I was quite certain I was not up to the task. It involved children and religion, I knew; I didn't know much about either. I was, after all, only studying to be a teacher. I was, perhaps, ready to assist someone else as I began the student teaching dimension of my studies. But me—would I stand alone with students to present the truths of the Catholic faith? No.

Then my professor, Sister Mariam, made it clear that she was not really just *asking* me. This being a catechist was, in fact, part of the required student teaching experience for our degree at this Catholic college. That was how in the end I said "Yes." Although I think I said something more like, "Okay, if I have to."

Was your "yes" to being a catechist as reluctantly spoken as mine? Or did you say an eager "yes" because you understood what I did not think about: that this is a continuation of the "yes" of baptism?

SAYING YES ISN'T EASY

As I was preparing to write this book, I attended the baptism of Ethan Alexander, the grandson of dear friends. As we stood around the baptismal pool, Father Ron blessed the water. The blessing tells the importance of water in salvation history: at creation the Holy Spirit breathed on the waters — the waters of the great flood ending sin and bringing new life, the waters of the Red Sea being parted so that the chosen people might escape from slavery and be set free, the waters of the Jordan River in which Jesus was baptized, and the water that flowed from his side as he hung on the cross. And then the prayer says, "After his resurrection, he told his disciples, 'Go out and teach all nations, baptizing them in the name in the name of the Father, and of the Son, and of the Holy Spirit.'"

I wonder if that "go out and teach" part of the prayer is why a lot of us cry when the water is poured over our heads. We are given the gift of grace. We become members of the church — and part of the church's mission to share the Good News of Jesus Christ.

I am not sure if I cried at my baptism, but I was close to tears when my first session as a catechist drew closer. Tears are sometimes another reminder of our baptism — Jesus didn't promise an easy life; he promised a meaningful life. The truth is, I wasn't just close to tears; I cried.

I had nightmares before that first class: I forgot to go; I was late and the kids were going wild when I arrived; I was there and no kids showed up; I was teaching and went to reach for the catechist guide, but instead of the guide there was an old, very heavy rubber tire. Maybe subconsciously that old tire symbolized a life preserver. It was there, but it would take some effort to use it!

The first class went off smoothly in spite of my fears. Then, as one of the fourth graders, Timmy, was leaving, he quietly told me I had done pretty good and then immediately asked when the real teacher would be coming.

I was now officially a catechist—ego deflated, but intact. I could do this. More, I felt called to do this. And so you have been called. Whether it was your pastor that issued the call or the director of catechesis or a friend—it is the Lord who calls you. And he graces you for your ministry. Beyond the fundamental vocation we received in baptism, the call to be a catechist is a special vocation, one affirmed by the church. "The call to the ministry of catechist is a vocation, an interior call, the voice of the Holy Spirit." (*National Directory for Catechesis*, p. 228; 54 B.8)

HARDLY A KNOW-IT-ALL

In one of the "007" movies, James Bond says, "I'm tempted to say yes immediately, but I think I'd maybe have a look around." I needed to "have a look around" when, years after my first experience as a catechist, I was settled in a new place and a new parish, and again the call to be a catechist came. This time I was asked to teach a particular religion topic that I did not know very well. So I asked our catechetical leader and then our pastor and a few other catechists. I realized it's okay not to know, not to have all the answers. I think one of the reasons—perhaps the first reason—the Lord calls us to be catechists is for our own growth in faith.

In *On Catechesis in Our Time* (*Catechesi Tradendae*) Pope John Paul II reminds us of the goal of catechesis: "The definitive aim of catechesis is to put people not only in touch, but also in communion and intimacy, with Jesus Christ" (#5). Bishop Ramirez, retired bishop of Las Cruces, New Mexico, said that the catechist is one who introduces people to Jesus Christ.

Therefore, he says, the catechist must know Jesus Christ and know the people. Jesus called you to be a catechist first so that you will grow closer to him and then so that you will help others to be his disciples.

Jesus' life was woven with water from his baptism in the Jordan to his many experiences at the Sea of Galilee. The first followers he called were fishermen and, Scripture says, he often withdrew to the sea. And he told his disciples they would be fishers of people: "catching" them, drawing them in closer.

We know the story of his baptism, when the Spirit of God came from the heavens like a dove and a voice from the heavens declared, "This is My beloved Son, with whom I am well pleased" (Matthew 3:17). When things were difficult for Jesus or when he was rejected, I wonder if he returned to the waters hoping to hear an echo of the Father's words and to feel the Spirit.

As a catechist, you will remind people that they are beloved children of God and temples of the Holy Spirit. You will be the reminder of their baptismal dignity and of God's embrace of them no matter what happens to them. That is what will "stick"—not how cleverly you taught or how many pages you covered in the text, but the knowledge, the conviction, that they are loved by God.

At Ethan's baptism, we sang the hymn "Come to the Water." The question at the end of the second verse struck me as I thought of you and all catechists: "Why should you spend your life except for the Lord?" No matter what the intervening reasons might be—it was a requirement for a degree, or your child will be in religious education this year, or the director is a friend of yours—you said yes because of the Lord. And you said yes because you know you can make a lasting difference.

THE CATECHIST'S LEGACY

It has been many years since I was a catechist for the first time. And it has been many years since I taught eighth graders at our parish and reclaimed my own confirmation. I have just recently moved back into the parish where I was a catechist for over ten years. After Mass one Sunday during Lent, Julia, the mother of one of the children I taught, approached me. "The eighth graders are going to reenact the Stations of the Cross this week. I have been working with them and I hope you can come to see them."

And so I went to see the eighth graders present the Living Stations of the Cross. Soon after they began I realized that they were using the script that I had written thirty-five years ago. There were some alterations to the performance: they began in the back of the church rather than the whole performance happening in the sanctuary; the costumes were more elaborate than the ones Sister Carolyn, our DRE, had sewn those years ago. But the words they spoke were the words I wrote. The words they spoke were the words that came to me as I reflected on each station and put pen to paper.

It was awesome! Somehow my teaching had lived on and my retelling of Jesus' story had endured. Some of the new performers were the children of the children I had taught. I had touched a generation who were not even born when I wrote the stations. And I was reminded of all those who had taught me about Jesus: my parents, my school teachers, the catechists—from Sister Jacqueline in first grade to Sister Mary Clare in eighth grade—my friends who taught me through their example, and so many others who touched me with Jesus' message along my life's journey. I thanked God for all those catechists.

I wondered, then, what else had lasted of what I had said or done as a catechist. I asked Jane, a former student and now a wife and mother, what she remembered. Jane said, "I remember that religion was important and that you catechists got along so well it felt like a community."

She paused. Then she said, "Yes, it was a real faith community, and learning about our faith was a key to happiness. And all of you catechists loved us. So we knew that God loved us too."

Jane didn't remember the book we used—though it was important for the content and to guide the learning and discussions. She didn't remember the tests we had but she does remember the prayers. Most of all, she wants her children to know what she learned: that God loves each of us and that we are a community of faith.

Those *are* the most important things. Those are the most important things that you will share as a catechist. There will be many other things you will teach about the Blessed Trinity and the Incarnation and the Resurrection and Pentecost. All of your teaching will enrich the discipleship of the young people entrusted to your care. And your teaching will influence generations not yet born because you have taught their parents or grandparents.

Author Joseph Campbell wrote, "The big question is whether you are going to be able to say a hearty yes to your adventure." You have said a "yes," though it may have been hesitant or it may have been more generous. Now, can it be a hearty—a heart-y—yes, filled with gratitude and grace?

⊛ *For reflection/action*

BEGINNER CATECHIST

Write down or enter on your computer/smartphone all the reasons you said yes to being a catechist. Keep this list and add to it through the year as you discover other reasons God called you to this ministry.

Choose one of the patron saints of catechists, like Saint Charles Borromeo, Saint Viator, Saint Robert Bellarmine, or another, to "adopt" as your patron and to whom you will pray for the strength and wisdom you need.

SEASONED CATECHIST

Reach out to one of the new catechists and offer an idea to help her or him get started.

Contact, by e-mail or phone or prayer, one of the people who taught you the faith; express your gratitude.

But I can't swim!

"Everyone jump in the lake!" This was a frightening command for me to hear as a young camp counselor. It was frightening for two reasons. One reason was that I could not swim—never learned. The other reason was that I was supposed to be the swimming instructor for the primary-age children at the camp.

I had been assigned my role that morning and was speechless. As a high school student I was too embarrassed to declare aloud what I knew to be true: "But I can't swim!" So, while I obeyed the camp director and stepped gingerly into the water, I was careful not to require too much of my "students"—or of myself—that first day.

Meanwhile, I placed a call to my friend Peg, an excellent swimmer who had been on the local golf club's swimming team. During our free time at camp and in the evenings when the campers were otherwise occupied, Peg sneaked in and taught me to swim. Each lesson she gave me I then taught to my little swimmers the next pool time. I was literally just a stroke ahead.

When I said yes to being a catechist, I had a similar experience. I was a little too embarrassed to admit after all my schooling in the faith that I didn't know—or didn't remember—what I would be required to teach. That's the main reason I had said no to being a catechist to begin with.

HOLY RELUCTANCE

We have many ancestors in faith who were just as reluctant to respond positively to God's call. There were prophets who objected to their call, like Jeremiah, who simply declared he was too young, or Isaiah, who claimed he was not worthy, or Jonah, who tried to escape by water.

In his book entitled *Just Build the Ark and the Animals will Come*, David Heller wrote about Luke, a ten-year-old, whose catechist asked him what God wanted Jonah to do. Luke answered, "God wanted him to be Jonah of Ark but he didn't want the fame and all the trouble that goes with it."

Maybe you and I don't want the fame and all the trouble either! The vocation of the catechist is to become a "public figure." People will now know you as one of the catechists, someone who teaches the faith. People might expect you to know all the answers. So, what excuses have you tried? "I am too young" or "too old"? "I am too busy" or just "I know someone who would be a better catechist"? Of course, if you are reading this book, at some point you realized no excuse was adequate and you finally gave in.

I think reluctance is probably the hallmark of a good catechist. At least it is the hallmark of a beginning catechist. That reluctance stems, I think, from a recognition of the critical nature of what a catechist is asked to do: proclaim the Good News of Jesus Christ and help the catechized to understand and to live the Catholic faith. There is a sense too of the immense richness of our faith and the profound mysteries of God's love, of our redemption, of the work of the Holy Spirit, of forgiveness and grace, of sacramental encounters, and of the reality of eternal life as our goal.

There is, too, an appreciation of the uniqueness of each child and that child's relationship with God, which makes us think, perhaps, that someone else—someone other than me—would surely be a more effective catechist. "Why me?" I asked when I received the invitation to be a catechist. And I kept hearing the reply, "Why not?"

When I became a parish director of religious education, the most important part of my job was to recruit catechists. Being on the inviting side, I can tell you it was not easy. But each day I would pray and remind God that this was his work, not mine. I would tell God that I had done all I could to get catechists, and now he had to help—send me people, and inspire them to say yes. Always, when we launched our catechetical program, we had all the catechists we needed. But I resent the comment "anyone can be a catechist." That is not true, and no one who recruits catechists believes it.

But you can be a catechist, a good catechist. I know that because you have been called by someone who sees in you gifts that only you can bring. Someone has seen in you gifts that are necessary for the message of Jesus to be heard and understood and responded to. The fact that you are somewhat unsure or that you are downright afraid only confirms that you are the right person.

Think of the Pentecost story. There were the apostles, gathered in the upper room, doors locked, afraid that what happened to Jesus might happen to them as well. They hear this driving wind and then see tongues of fire resting on each other. I can't help but think that, initially at least, this wind and fire were not particularly a comfort to their fears and uncertainty. Yet, almost immediately, they are courageous and able to go out and proclaim.

Pentecost seems to me to indicate that fear and uncertainty might just be the threshold the Holy Spirit prefers. Rather than the confidence of unlocked doors and open windows and the easy comings and goings of "I know what I'm doing," maybe the Spirit looks for the places where we are unsure, a little lost, or—to stick with our water analogies—in "over our heads."

I really don't know any catechist worth her or his salt who was totally confident and self-assured when beginning this ministry. Then the Pentecost moments can come; then the Spirit sees our need and comes in wind that moves us along, in fire that warms us and melts our fears, and in the inspiration to speak the precise word that some child needs to hear.

J.R.R. Tolkien wrote, "It does not do to leave a live dragon out of calculations if you live near him." The Spirit's coming did not end all of the reasons the apostles had to be anxious. It did, however, strengthen them to face those challenges. There may still be dragons nearby, or deep sea monsters that haunt our dreams or seem to be in our class on a particular day. But the Holy Spirit is there too—helping us all along. We can be realistic about the difficulties of catechizing young people, but not incapacitated by them.

There are difficulties, and these may lead us to make objections to being a catechist, as some of the prophets did. You may be young, but that means you can bring energy and enthusiasm to this ministry. You may be older, but then you also have the wisdom that comes from living your faith through the years. You may not be an orator, but you have words of comfort and encouragement that you can offer your class. You may lack outstanding talents, but you have all that is necessary: love for God, love for those you teach, faithfulness in your own discipleship, a commitment to growth.

CATECHIST AS EVANGELIZER

Because you were called, I am certain that you have the qualities of an evangelist. That is why someone would have spotted you as a good potential catechist. Pope Paul VI's document *Evangelization in the Modern World* (*Evangelii Nuntiandi*) names the crucial qualities an evangelizer must have.

The first is witness of life. It is logical that unless we believe and live by what we are teaching, we will not be believable. We are also to be always working for unity: with and among our students, in our parish, with other Christians, with all people of good will. We are to serve the truth. Always we proclaim the truth, even when we do not quite measure up to all that Jesus asks. An evangelizer, and a catechist too, must be animated first by love—not a desire to change others, or to argue them out of their beliefs, but to love them. Finally, we are to approach our proclaiming of the Good News with "the fervor of the saints," that is, with the passion and urgency with which they shared the faith (EN #76-80).

There is a quotation attributed to various authors that says:

> *"When you come to the edge*
> *of all the light you have known*
> *and are about to step out*
> *into the darkness,*
> *faith is knowing*
> *one of two things will happen:*
> *there will be something solid*
> *to stand on, or*
> *you will be taught how to fly."*

I have found that quote to be true in all my years as a catechist. Just when it seemed darkest and the road disappeared, it was then I would be given the solid footing of practical help or the wings of a creative idea.

TEACHERS WHO LEARN

When the camp director shouted "Everyone in the lake" on my first day as swim instructor, all I could do was stay focused on small swim-like things that I could do and that would not endanger my little flock of swimmers. So, as new catechists, we have to begin slowly, doing what we are comfortable with and what will help the students and keep them safe.

Then we have to find our own swim instructor. Someone who will be a coach for us or something that will enable us to employ a new "stroke" each day to keep the students engaged. Maybe you need help with classroom management. Maybe you are not comfortable praying with the students. Maybe you need a lesson in how to begin and how to facilitate group work or how to make use of the catechist guide. Maybe you want to incorporate a DVD and need some help with choosing an appropriate one, or help with how to introduce and follow up when you view a DVD. Be on the lookout for the right teacher for the information or skill you need to learn. Don't only look at other catechists—although they may be a great help. Your family and friends may have expertise to share. Your own former catechists may be able to help, or you may get insights just by reflecting on how they taught you. Maybe a school teacher who teaches the same-age children as those you are catechizing can offer clues into what works with children of that age.

Just like me learning to swim a stroke ahead of the campers, all we need right now is how to do the very next lesson as effectively as we can, making it a little more engaging than last week's lesson. As I learned just one simple thing from Peg at each of my swim lessons, just focus on learning one "stroke" you can apply in the next class. Maybe it's a new way to begin the class or a way to check in the middle of class to be sure they are "getting it," or a new way to end with a sense of purpose for the students for the week ahead.

There is no need for us to declare "But I can't swim"—or "I can't teach"—for we are all learners. As long as we keep learning and we're a stroke ahead, we can lead the way!

 *For reflection/action*

BEGINNER CATECHIST

Make a list of the five things you want most to learn in order to be a better catechist. As you prepare for the next class, what do you need most to learn? Who might be able to teach you what you need to learn? Contact that person and make a plan to learn from him or her.

Reflect on the gifts you do bring to being a catechist, rather than focusing on what you may not bring. Help your students to name the gifts they have.

SEASONED CATECHIST

Write down two of your best ideas for teaching a successful class. Share these ideas with a new catechist or exchange them with another seasoned catechist for two of her or his ideas.

Be on the lookout for a catechist or a student who seems to be saying "But I can't swim." Offer help.

Stick your toe in

I often visit a friend who lives on the Gulf Coast. Walking the beach, I pass parents teaching their children to swim. It is, for the most part, a very gradual process. There is occasionally a day when the waves are immense, and then the need to swim intensifies so the lessons are more intense. But precluding the whitecaps, learning to swim takes time. And so it should be for learning to be a catechist.

When I became a parish director of religious education for the first time, it was in a brand-new parish. I was to begin the programs that would be offered. The well-intentioned pastor wanted to help me understand my role, so he brought me to visit the director at the neighboring parish, which had been established many years before. Besides being established, it was also an enormous parish both in terms of its geographical area and the number of people it served.

I went to visit the lovely DRE, who was eager to share all that she was doing in her parish. She was directing the children's program, the youth ministry, the Rite of Christian Initiation of Adults, the adult Scripture study, and the new moms' prayer and play group. She was doing even more than that, but as she went on describing it all, I had reached the capacity for comprehension in my head. It was all too much, and I left feeling overwhelmed and inadequate and certain that I had to resign.

My pastor calmed me down. I was thinking he expected me to do what that experienced, competent DRE was doing. I thought I was supposed to "dive in" when I didn't have a clue how to swim.

Too often our eager new catechists may feel they have to dive in. Don't do it! Like the child learning to swim, all that is necessary is to stick your toe in at first. The rest will come later.

WHO WILL I BE FOR THEM?

Whenever I began a new year as a catechist, I would find myself thinking about the catechists who taught me about Jesus. Specifically, I tried to recall who taught me when I was the age of the children I was about to teach. Who taught you? What did they teach you? Pay attention to what it is that you remember.

I have met with catechists and asked them these questions. Most of what they remember is not what the catechist taught or what the catechist did, but who the catechist was—the qualities that had a lasting effect on them. "She was so kind!" "Our third-grade catechist was fun—we learned a lot and we loved going to class." "He really cared about us; you could tell because he always listened to us."

The first step in being a good catechist is not about what you will do but about who you will *be*—with and for the children, youth, or adults you will catechize. Who you are, who you will be for them, flows, of course, from your own discipleship. Jesus calls us, as his disciples, to be loving, to be forgiving, to be inclusive of the outcast. These are the qualities that will be remembered when someone years from now asks them what you—their catechist—were like.

There are a few water experiences I have had that parallel my experiences of learning to be a catechist. First, when I was a child, my parents had a friend who owned a sailboat. Mr. Bergman was an excellent sailor and would teach us about manning the jib and paying attention to what the wind was doing. The whole principle of sailing is to work with the wind. So, when we seemed to be going in the opposite direction of our goal, Mr. Bergman would say, "Sometimes you gotta go this-a-way to get that-a-way." In the same way, the quickest, most direct way may not be the way to achieve the goal of forming disciples. Most importantly, as catechists, we have to pay attention to the wind that is the Holy Spirit, the principal agent of catechesis. The Spirit knows where we need to go and what the best way to get there is.

A second experience I remember involving water was when my husband, Ray, our son Nick, and my mom and I went on a cruise. When we came near the Yucatan Peninsula, there was an optional tour to the Mayan ruins. I decided to go and was excited to take the smaller boat that would launch from our large ship. I learned that the small boat was nearly overcome by the waves that didn't even faze the large ship. I was afraid, which I had not been on the big boat. I was keenly aware of being separated from the other people with whom I had been journeying. I realized then, and I realized again when I was a catechist, the power of the community of faith to weather rough seas and to assuage our fears. Staying close to shore may be reinterpreted as "stay on the big ship"—stay close to the community of faith, to the community of catechists who share the challenges you face and can be resources to help you journey safely.

Having reflected on who we want to be with the children, how else can we "stick our toes in" to this ocean of catechesis? Maybe the next question to reflect on is, "Who are these children I am to teach?"

If you are able, try just observing children who are the age of the children you will be teaching. Maybe a friend of yours has children that age, or there are children that age in your extended family. Just spend time watching and listening. Ask them about what they like to do and what they don't like. What do they play with and how do they treat each other? What bothers them? Ask questions; their answers will give you a sense of what is important to them, what they worry about, and what they hope for. And those things will help you connect the message of Jesus to their real lives.

Author Ray Bradbury, in *Zen and the Art of Writing*, wrote: "And, after all, isn't that what life is all about, the ability to go around the back and come up inside of other people's heads to look out at the foolish miracle and say, 'Oh, so that's how you see it! Well now, I must remember that!'" We have to remember who we are teaching and to see things, not from our adult point of view, but from their point of view if we are to connect the word of God with what they know and feel and what counts in their lives now.

It is so important to make use of your catechist guide! It provides information and guidance to teach the lesson and it leads you to other resources that are invaluable. In your guide you will see that each catechetical lesson has certain key elements: prayer, content from Scripture and Catholic Tradition, connection with the child's life experience, a call to live out what we have learned. These are the essential dimensions of the lesson and are aimed at the children's minds as they learn more about Jesus and the church; they are aimed at the children's hearts as their love for God—Father, Son, and Holy Spirit—grows; they are aimed at the children's behaviors—faith changes the way in which we live.

FIRST STEPS

So, here's how I stuck my toes in to learn how to be a catechist: First, I prayed. I prayed for the insights and inspiration I would need to share the message, and I prayed for the children. A friend told me about an elderly nun she knew. My friend was walking past this sister's classroom and saw the sister kneeling on the floor by one of the desks. My friend thought the sister had fallen and went in to help her. But, it turns out, the sister was intentionally kneeling, as difficult as it was for her to get down and get back up again. The sister told my friend that she would kneel beside each desk and pray for the child who would sit there. Pray for each child, thinking about what each child needs.

Next, I would go to the guide and read the lesson background that would help me to understand on an adult level the content I would be teaching. The guide also tells what materials you will need. So I would check the materials needed and be sure I had them, or that the catechetical leader or principal would have them for me.

Then I would prepare the lesson, reading it over, seeing what questions and activities the children would be asked to do. Sometimes the guide offers options for a lesson's activities and, once I knew my class, I could choose the option that would best suit them.

Depending on the guide is a good way to stick our toes in and begin. But there was something the guide didn't tell me that first time I was a catechist. It didn't tell me the importance—the critical importance—of being on time for class, of being the first one to arrive. On one or two occasions, I came after a few of the kids were already there, and I realized that whoever is there first sets the tone for the class. The tone should be set by the catechist, and I made sure from then on that I was there first.

Being there first has other benefits too. Obviously it is better than running in at the last minute and not being able to collect my thoughts. But being there first, standing at the door to welcome my students, I was able to catch their moods and to ask how things were going in their lives. I began to learn who was on what team and to ask about their games. I learned about which child was having a hard time in school or at home and who needed additional encouragement during class. Being there first, I set the tone and got information that helped me to connect our lesson to what was happening in their lives.

When a child is learning to swim and the teacher says, "Just stick your toe in," the child will gradually put a foot in. When a wave comes and the child is unexpectedly met with new depth of waters, the child may suddenly run out of the water and retreat for awhile. Take it slowly, catechist! If you find yourself getting overwhelmed, retreat a bit and try a simpler approach next lesson—play music while they work independently instead of trying group work.

If a child learning to swim sticks toes in and then a foot and then walks in further, the swim teacher may say, "Now put your face in the water and blow bubbles!" The wonder and the laughter that ensue can be mesmerizing. This child, once reluctant to stick a toe in, is now enjoying new depth. You will get to the new depth when you are ready and it should be fun—for you and your students.

One day I was walking along a beach where the waves were enormous and whitecapped. Out in the water was a father holding his small child who was only two years at the most. As the waves crashed over both of them, the father would jump and laugh and the drenched child would laugh too. Two lessons for catechists: one is that the Father holds you. The other lesson is that if we adults enjoy the lesson, so will the students.

And always, the Father who holds us is there and wants us to succeed in our mission, which is his work. Some years ago a friend sent me an e-mail with a survey. This survey was to ascertain my satisfaction—not with a store or company, but with God's service. It was entitled "God wants to know" and asked questions like, "Do you have any suggestions for improving the quality of God's service?"

We might laugh at this idea at first, but then didn't Jesus say, "Ask and it will be given to you; seek and you will find; knock and the door will be opened to you" (Matthew 7:7)? Stick your toe in, ask for the help you need, and enjoy the water!

✸ *For reflection/action*

BEGINNER CATECHIST

Look at your catechist guide to see what resources it contains. Go through the guide to prepare your next lesson using all the helps the guide offers.

Go back in this chapter and review the essential dimensions of a lesson. Which of those dimensions is easiest for you? Go a little deeper with that element in the next class. For example, if you are most comfortable with presenting Scripture, tell the Scripture story instead of just reading it. If you are most comfortable with prayer, try inviting the children to pray spontaneously instead of saying a memorized prayer, or vice versa.

SEASONED CATECHIST

Sometimes as experienced catechists, we can latch on to

something that "worked" and never again experiment with a new approach. Pretend you are a beginner again and stick your toe in to a new way of doing a lesson.

Reflect on the joy and laughter that happens with your class. When was the last time you laughed together? Make sure it happens at the next class.

Stay close to shore

The little child who has just learned to swim a bit can be overly confident and be tempted to venture out a bit too far. There are, hopefully, adults who are nearby and able to spring into action when the wandering gets too deep. So, as I pass family gatherings on my beach walks, I frequently hear one of the elders call out to a child who is entering the water, "Don't go out too far! Stay close to the shore!"

It is good advice, to stay close to shore, to be careful lest we be engulfed. This is true especially as we learn to swim or learn to be a catechist—don't go out further than we can handle. It is important for an effective lesson that we not wander too far beyond our "secure zone"—that area where I am comfortable enough to function well.

As I pointed out in the last chapter, the catechist guide is an invaluable tool that helps us stay close to shore. While we don't want to be locked in forever to the lesson steps in the guide, it is a secure place to begin. And the guide is a jumping-off point to try—a little at a time—some new things. We can go a little deeper each lesson, but taking it easy so we are still feeling secure as we teach.

I always divided up my planning into three sections: what to do before they get to class, what to do when they are in class, and what to do after they leave class. Each of these three parts is key in our effectiveness as catechists.

BEFORE THEY COME

First, what do you need to do before class? Go to your guide to prepare the lesson. A good catechist guide will give you a sense of the developmental stage of the children you are to teach and how to meet them where they are. Lessons in a good text are constructed to speak to children of a particular age and to relate to their lives through examples and activities. You don't need to do it all—stay close to shore and use the guide.

The guide will tell you that young children are still egocentric but growing toward recognizing others' rights. Matching each of them with a partner to accomplish a task might be a good idea. Young children also have a short attention span, so varying the lesson approach can be helpful in retaining their interest. For example, "Let's move our chairs into a circle to hear this story about Jesus...Now move your chairs back, and tell me about what Jesus did when he saw Zacchaeus in the tree."

For intermediate children, their peer group takes on greater importance. Consider what task they can do cooperatively with a small group. For example, "We just read about baptism. Now let's act out what happens at a baptism."

Junior high young people seem to be the highest energy people on the planet! Have them move—engage their energy. Have them visit the younger children's class to teach those children something they have learned about Advent or Lent or to teach them a prayer.

The guide will help you with who the children are and how to craft the lesson. It will provide valuable resources (including online resources) and give you a clear goal for the lesson you are teaching. With the information and plans it provides, the guide can help you stay close to shore as a catechist.

When I was a catechist, before the children came I remembered what I had learned about the children I was teaching—their developmental stages and their life experiences. I thought about what may have happened lately: maybe their team lost a big tournament or maybe there was a death in one of their families or maybe we are meeting right before Christmas break. How could I make reference to what has happened in their lives and make a connection with the content of the lesson? (Also, make sure you know the time frame of classes. One of my catechists thought we had only 45 minutes when we really had an hour. Another thought we had an hour and a half. You will get used to what "fits" in the length of time you are given and be able to adjust as you prepare—skipping a question, or adding an additional two or three questions or an activity you have devised to reinforce the lesson.)

Then I used the guide to choose optional activities or questions. I had one group that always gave one-word answers, even though the guide said the discussion would take fifteen minutes. I was left wondering what to do with the other fourteen minutes and fifty-nine seconds. In order to "stay close to shore," I had to plan to fill that time and not be left with nothing to do! I would make up several more questions or give them time to think up questions that they could ask the class.

In reading over the lesson, I also thought about what experiences or stories I had that related to the content of the lesson. Maybe the chapter was about the fourth commandment and I could share ways I showed respect for my mom as she grew older; maybe the chapter was about God's creation and I could tell about the environmental group to which my neighbor belonged. The question is, what does this lesson remind you of in your life? What does this lesson remind you of that you have experienced or seen in a movie or read about or heard on the news? And all of this preparing can be done in half an hour or less—not long to ensure a good lesson.

One of the lessons I learned from my students is that I had better be sure they know the vocabulary used in the lesson. Most texts will define new faith words but we have to know what words may be new to our students that might not be presented as new vocabulary. New vocabulary can also be a quick review when students are asked to use the word in a sentence about the lesson.

WHEN THEY ARE IN CLASS

If I had prepared well, then I could be secure when my students arrived for class. I would be at the door to greet them and I would be confident that I knew the lesson and where I was going in teaching it. Staying close to the shore means continuing to learn about my students too. It was somewhat frustrating to me to only meet these children once a week. I began composing open-ended sentences for them to complete as we gathered. These statements, when completed by them, gave me further insights into their thoughts and lives and into their knowledge of and feelings about their faith. Some statements I have used are:

> *I come to class because...*
> *If I met Jesus today he'd tell me...*
> *If I wrote my autobiography a good title would be...*
> *Lately I have begun to realize...*
> *My friends think...*
> *I would be great if only...*
> *If I could change one thing in my life I would...*

What really scares me is...
One question I'd like to get answered is...

With younger children you might simply ask them for a word they remember from the lesson, or have them complete a statement orally: "I am happy when..." or "My favorite part of our lesson was..." "I want to tell Jesus..."

The ending of a lesson is just as important as the greeting at the door and the lesson itself.

The difference with a religion class, as opposed to other classes they may have in school, is that this subject is supposed to be lived. God's gift of faith is freely given but calls for a response. Send them forth with a mission to accomplish during the week. It may be one you assign. For example: "This week we learned that Jesus taught: 'Blessed are the peacemakers' (Matthew 5:9). Do one thing to be a peacemaker this week." Or each student might decide on her or his own mission: "Given what we learned in this class, what mission will you accomplish for Jesus this week?"

When you gather the next week, be sure to ask about their mission and what each of them did to live the lesson. This sharing of the mission—in which you should share what you did too—can be a quick review as well, alerting you as to what may need to be reinforced.

AFTER THEY LEAVE

When your children leave class, your work continues. Spend some time reflecting on how the session went. Were the students paying attention? Were they engaged and responsive? Was there any disruption? If so, why did it happen? Maybe you lectured instead of getting them involved; maybe you had them work in groups but the task wasn't clear or you gave too much time to the task. If we ask ourselves what went wrong and why and then apply those insights, we can improve with every lesson—still staying close to shore, but gradually moving a little further away.

BE NOT AFRAID

Another water story serves to illustrate the importance of staying close to shore. My friends Peg and Lynn and I were visiting Lynn's aunt and uncle. One afternoon, we went swimming in Lake Decatur. We were jumping in off the floating dock and tossing a beach ball around and generally having a great time. At one point, Lynn swam away to fetch the beach ball. Suddenly she panicked. She was flailing wildly and screaming, "Help, I'm drowning!" Peg and I laughed uncontrollably, trying to get the words out that we wanted to shout to Lynn. She continued to scream as I was finally able to blurt out the message that would save our friend: "Just stand up, Lynn! Put your feet down!" The water was, in fact, little more than waist-high.

Sometimes we think we are drowning; sometimes we believe we have wandered very far from shore. Perhaps a lesson went badly. Perhaps the students were less than receptive. There is no catechist who has not had this experience on occasion. Maybe we are in too deep, but we can stand up and get control again. We can call out and someone will tell us how to save ourselves—what we can do better next time. If we have been conscientious and prepared, we have the "water wings" to preserve us. We will be used to reflecting on how the lesson went and assessing what we can do better next time. We aren't really in over our heads.

There is a Native American saying that goes like this: "Now is a rushing river. There are those who would hug the shore, but there is no shore. Push off into the stream. Hold your head above the foray. See who else is in the midst of things and celebrate."

Even when we have moments of panic, we can be sure that the catechists who have gone before us panicked too—even the catechist-saints were once beginners. We can take ourselves so seriously that we are caught up in the thought that we might drown—though the water is not deep. Let's celebrate staying close to shore until we are ready to swim away.

 *For reflection/action*

BEGINNER CATECHIST

Focus on one of the three parts of your next lesson. What will you do before the children come? When they are there? When they have gone?

When have you panicked about being a catechist? Why? How can you avoid panicking again? Who can you count on to help you?

Invite someone to observe you teaching and to offer pointers for improving your skills.

SEASONED CATECHIST

How do you depend on the wind that is the Holy Spirit? Pray to the Holy Spirit for all catechists.

What evidence is there that you connect to the larger faith

community? What gift do you bring to that community and its catechetical ministry?

Sometimes we get comfortable with old lesson plans when we could try a new approach. Invite someone to observe you teaching and to offer pointers for improving your skills and trying something new.

Never swim alone
(and you never do)

One of the first rules of learning to swim is never swim alone. Parent after parent on the beach can be heard calling to their little ones, "Wait for me. Stop there."

As a catechist, you never do swim alone in your catechetical sessions because the students are swimming with you. Some of them are brand-new at this too; some have never attended classes before. You have to let them know they don't swim alone either. One or more of your students may only be able to come to every other class due to family situations, or health issues may make their attendance sporadic. Let them stick a toe in too, let them stay close to shore, and let them work with a partner who has been in class longer and more regularly. You are swimming with them, all of them, so don't leave even one behind. That's what they will remember—that you let no one struggle alone, that you let no one drown.

When I was about seven, our family went on vacation to my parents' friends' house in Lake Geneva, Wisconsin. My older brothers, Bob and Dick, were able to go on the powerboat to water ski. My parents deemed me too young. I am sure I cried.

To appease me, their friends offered to let me take out their dinghy, complete with a five-horsepower motor, all by myself. I dutifully donned the life vest and boarded my own private yacht. It was glorious! I was in control, independent, master of my journey. It was fun until I traveled far from the shore and the motor sputtered and died. Now there was no one to help me, no one to tell me what to do or to restart the motor for me.

SWIMMING BUDDIES

You don't swim alone because, hopefully, you have a director or a pastor who ensures you have the formation and in-service to assure your success. During my first stint as a DRE, I didn't know enough to realize what the catechists should have been able to expect from me. Our pastor was also brand-new at pastoring and this was the first time he was inaugurating a religious education program. We got better at supporting our catechists in the second year. You can turn to your DRE, principal, pastor, associate pastor, or deacon to ask your questions about the content of lessons or to seek help with ways to explain the truths of the faith to students. Someone on the pastoral staff may be able to suggest supplementary resources you might use, such as a good DVD on the Mass or a book on the saints or a website that would be appropriate for students of the age you teach.

Who else swims with you—or might be asked to swim along? Certainly, parents and guardians can be enlisted through take-home activities and the use of websites related to your texts and lesson topics. Parents can also be invited to share their faith as part of your class. One of my students had a father who was an orthopedic surgeon. This doctor went to a third-world country every other year and was a perfect guest speaker to invite when we studied Catholic social teaching. Who are the parents of your students? What gifts and experiences do they have that can enrich your class?

A pastoral staff member may have a particular love for the Eucharist and can speak when you study the Mass; instead of reading about deacons, invite the deacon in to talk about his ministry. Who are the other leaders who head up parish organizations? What might they bring to the *swim*? Who are the other catechists? You are a swim team, after all. Perhaps one of the other catechists has a special devotion to Mary while you are devoted to Saint Francis of Assisi, and you could swap classes to share your devotions.

I remember teaching my student sixth graders many ways to pray: the memorized prayers of the community, prayer with Scripture, spontaneous prayer, meditation. When they asked me if we could try meditating using yoga postures, I replied that my body was not able to do yoga postures. But my friend Mary Beth did yoga, so I invited her to pray with us.

The additional benefit of your swimming with these other folks — fellow catechists, parish leaders, parents, friends — is that when you invite them into the swim, they swim with your students too. Your students are then forming other relationships that can strengthen their faith and assure them they never swim alone.

STUDENT SWIMMERS AND YOU

You assure the students that they do not swim alone when you demonstrate that you understand their lives, their joys and sorrows, and their hopes and challenges. You companion them when you are aware of the socioeconomic realities of the area, the educational level, even the political climate. The more you know about the students and their lives, the better equipped you will be to identify the seeds of the gospel that are already present as well as those "weeds" that are counter to gospel values and how the gospel message can invite transformation.

Your own comfort with the lesson will allow you to be comfortable with the students, and that relationship is key to the learning that takes place. This lesson was one that I learned when I took a post-graduate course in public policy for non-profit organizations. The young professor was clearly unprepared and uncomfortable. His teaching style was to turn his back to us and write on the chalkboard while reading his lecture to us. If anyone tried to ask a question, the professor mocked the questioner. We students were all adults who were holding responsible positions in our various institutions. Yet, when we were so poorly treated by this "teacher," we became vengeful. When break time came, we left the room quickly, complaining about the professor's dearth of methodology and lack of respect for us students. Then we vowed not to return to class when break was over until he came to get us. We were, in fact, swimming alone as far as the professor was concerned, and so we sought to swim with each other.

Learning didn't happen in that class. The erosion of the teacher-student relationship made it impossible to focus on anything except our anger. The university offered us the opportunity to take the course again, tuition-free, with a different professor. It all started with an insecure teacher who was unwilling to prepare his classes.

Your relationship with your students is of prime importance in the catechetical process. That relationship can flourish when you get the help you need—when you recognize that you do not swim alone and you take advantage of the resources and assistance available.

When I had gained some experience as a director, catechists would sometimes approach and ask for help with "controlling" their class. Behavioral issues were arising and, wisely, the catechists sought solutions. I would go to observe such a class before offering any advice. Inevitably I would find that the children were not engaged in the lesson—they were sitting and looking at their books while the catechist read the lesson to them. Or each child was given a paragraph to read and so could count the paragraphs ahead, identify their own paragraph, and tune out until their turn came.

These catechists, like my professor, were swimming alone and leaving the students behind. For all the catechists' wonderful intentions and generosity, the students' energies were undirected, and so they began to find ways to amuse themselves. The catechist in this sort of class would be discouraged, at wit's end really. The catechist recognized that he or she was swimming alone and wanted the students to come!

Here is one of the questions I began to pose whenever I worked with catechists: "How necessary are the students to your lesson?" If you are lecturing, or their engagement is limited to the paragraph each one is to read, then they are not very necessary, are they? How do we craft our lesson so that they are not only engaged but so that the lesson cannot go on without them? When they are swimming with us there is no time for them to get distracted or to cause a disruption.

The *National Directory for Catechesis* names some elements of human methodology—ways that people learn (NDC pp. 95-105; #29, A-H). We can use some of these elements to be sure the children are immersed in the lesson. One element is that people learn through experience. How can we provide an experience of the lesson?

Maybe the lesson is about Jesus' teaching to love one another. A catechist might have partners work together or form small groups to do a task—answer a question together or compose a haiku about Jesus' teaching. The real lesson, though, is that the catechist then asks, not about what they accomplished, but about how well they worked with their partners or group. Were they loving, in that they contributed to the task and respected other's contributions?

Another lesson might be about ways to pray. Instead of reading about the ways, compose a brief prayer for each kind of prayer and pray the prayers together. Then have students choose one kind of prayer to compose their own. Younger students can just pray their prayer and perhaps their classmates can name the kind of prayer it is.

One of the other elements of methodology is learning by heart. Memorizing a prayer or a line from Scripture embeds it in our memory. Class times are normally too brief to do the memorizing then, but students can choose a Scripture to memorize, learn it at home, and share it in class. This exercise also engages the family, which is another element of methodology.

Other elements, like learning within the Christian community, happen naturally in class through partners, group work, skits, and discussions. And all of these keep children engaged. We swim together; we learn together; everyone is busy doing her or his part—and then there is no energy left over for causing any trouble.

Theologian Rosemary Haughton wrote, "Satan's plausible suggestion is that if we want good things we must make sure we keep them for ourselves. Someone else might take them. But Noah's ark is the sign that we can only be saved together."

My small boat experience taught me this lesson: I needed other people sometimes; certainly as a catechist I needed other people. One of the gifts of the community is that it helps us to discern what we need to do. One is never certain if what one hears at sea is the voice of God calling us to growth, or sirens luring us, as they did the mythological mariners, to destruction. The community, those with whom we swim, keeps us attentive to Scripture, Tradition, and the living witness of the faithful. And those things make us better catechists and remind us that Jesus swims with us too—or rather, as his catechists, we swim with him.

Rabbi David Wolpe wrote, "It is human voices which save us, that throw us the rope to tug us back to shore." Don't swim alone. Remember you never do.

 *For reflection/action*

BEGINNER CATECHIST

Look around your parish. Who are the people who can be a resource for you? Ask one of them to help with an idea for your next lesson.

Think about the parents and guardians of your children. How will you invite them to be involved? Are there parent pages in the texts you can ask them to do with their children? Is there a website with resources for families you can direct them to?

SEASONED CATECHIST

Think about the resource people you have used to assist you as a catechist. To inspire other catechists, write an article for the parish bulletin or website about these people.

Make a list of the various DVDs, books, websites you have found helpful in your catechizing. Share the list with your fellow catechists. Try a new resource and add it to the list.

Wanna go deeper?

When I was in grade school, my friend Donna's family had a cottage on Paw Paw Lake in Michigan. Donna invited me to their cottage to stay for a few days. One of the experiences I anticipated with tremendous excitement was the chance to learn to water ski.

The day came for my initiation into the sport of water skiing, and Donna and her brother and his friend gave me instructions. I would be in the water near the pier when we took off. I was to get in position: ski tips up and parallel, tow rope firmly in hand. The final instruction they shouted was, "Never let go of the rope!"

Unfortunately, the boat had only a fifteen horsepower motor, hardly enough to pull me up. So I obediently clung to the rope and I gradually went totally under the water. "Don't let go of the rope," I kept repeating to myself as I held my breath and skied along the lake's sanded bottom.

At last, out of breath, I let go of the rope and surfaced. My friends greeted my sputtering with, "Why didn't you let go?" Sometimes holding on saves us; sometimes letting go saves us. And we continue this rhythm of holding on and letting go as we grow into our catechetical ministry, never finishing the growth but rather moving on to a different level of ability.

So maybe by now you are ready to go deeper. You can now let go of the guide a bit and try some news ways to involve your students in learning and, more importantly, learning to live their faith.

In the Gospel of Luke, we read about the disciple-fishermen who had "worked hard all night and caught nothing." Jesus was in their boat teaching and when he had finished he said to the disciples, "Put out into deep water and let down your nets for a catch." Does Jesus ask us, too, his catechists, to go deeper? Are you ready to respond to "hook" your students?

A LITTLE DEEPER

An easy place to begin is to enhance the environment for the lesson. If you have not yet set a prayer space, do that. Get a simple cloth of the color of the current liturgical season, a Bible, and perhaps a battery-operated candle. Consider what the coming lesson is about and what symbol you might bring: if the lesson is on the beatitudes, go online and print out a picture of the mount where Jesus taught them; if the lesson is on creation, bring a flower; if it is on the sacraments, bring some oil in a beautiful container for the prayer space.

Another practice you might try is the use of open-ended sentences at the end of class. Like the open-ended statements I used at the beginning of class that helped me to know the children better, the ones I used at the end helped me to know what I needed to address in our next class. The students could choose any one of these statements to complete. But they couldn't choose the same one every week! Here are the ones I used:

> *I learned...*
> *I remembered...*

It surprised me that...
I want to learn more about...
This week I will...

Younger children can complete the statement orally, or you might have them share one "special" word from the lesson that they will remember.

As you get to know your students better, you will know which activities in the guide they will enjoy doing and which will just not work with them. Each group I taught had a "group personality" which included what most engaged them and what they rebelled against. Some groups love role-playing to tell the story in a lesson; others like making up a song or a poem in response to a lesson. If you find you don't really know what they like to do, ask them.

How do you begin a lesson? Is it always routine, or do you vary your approach to keep the students' interest? When preparing a lesson, ask yourself about what current event relates to the topic of the lesson. Can you open with a story from the news? Can you bring an appropriate "prop" to pique their curiosity? I brought a magnifying glass to one class session and introduced a section on morality with the idea of "examining" our decisions.

BEYOND THE BOOK
What are the ways we can go "beyond the book" to add depth to the lesson and increase the students' involvement in their faith? Here are ways I found successful.

• Divide the chapter into sections and assign each section to student partners. Have them summarize their section for the class. (Be sure to add any points they missed or to correct any errors.) Give the partners time to ask a question for their classmates to answer.

- Instead of using a story found in your text, use a real-life story.

- Have each student illustrate one page of the chapter. Then put them in order as a mural and have each student explain their illustration.

- Have a guest speaker or a panel. (Be sure to follow your parish policies for guests in class.) Instead of reading about lay ecclesial ministers, invite a lay minister to tell his or her story; instead of reading about the Catholic belief in the sacredness of all life, invite the leaders of your respect life group to present a panel covering the critical life issues they are helping to address.

- Use a DVD or online video that expresses the lesson's message. Be sure to prepare an introduction and a follow-up to ensure that the students are focusing on the message. You might want to direct their viewing: listen for the decision that Sara has to make. What steps does she take before making her decision? For younger students, you might say, "Watch the story of Max and Maddie's argument. What could each of them have done differently to avoid fighting?"

- Have students prepare a presentation to share with younger students what they have learned. They might do a skit or a puppet show. This works well with the seasons of the church year, since the younger students learn about those too.

- Your students could make a booklet covering a topic (a Scripture story, a saint story, a sacrament) they are studying. The booklets could then be shared with younger children or with the students' families. It would be even better if they leave the last page blank and invite their family to add to the booklet and bring it back to class to share.

- Design a class board game to use as a review. At the end of each chapter, have students write new questions.

- Bring in newspapers or magazines or check for appropriate websites, and ask students to find stories that express the theme of the lesson.

- In preparation for a lesson, have students write questions and interview a parent or other family member, or a friend or parish leader. This can serve as the introduction to a lesson. Or children can do interviews after they have finished a lesson and bring in their reports to review the lesson.

STILL DEEPER

Want to go deeper? Keep track of ways you approach lessons and activities you use, so that you can intentionally change the experience of a class for your children. I always kept a one-page calendar with just a few lines for each month of our religious education year. I would jot down what I used for each lesson so I could be sure I varied the classes and kept the students' interest.

On that same calendar, I saved the last lines of each month to put in the names of four students. Each week I would choose one of those names and focus a bit more on that student, offering that one affirmation and encouragement. I realized early on that it is easy to focus on the more outgoing, verbal students and to be inattentive to the quiet and shy ones. My calendar ensured I would not forget even the quietest student and that I would "go deeper" in relating to each one as they grew in their discipleship to Jesus.

Going deeper in our catechizing means analyzing our successful dives too. What was it that worked and why did it work? Maybe we initially think the fact that we asked the students to do a report for a lesson was what "worked." But upon closer examination, we see that it was working with a partner that really got the students' energy up. Sharing successes with other catechists, and they with us, can be most helpful in our efforts to go deeper.

A good source for ways to go deeper is catechists who have "retired" and are no longer teaching. They may have been teaching for many years and just need a break, or they may have grown older and no longer have the energy to work with young people. They may have an infirmity that precludes their being able to drive to class or to go upstairs to a classroom. See if there is such a catechist in your area who is willing to mentor you into the depths.

When Jesus told the disciples to "go deeper," they were safely in a boat. (See Matthew 14:22-32.) The situation was very different when the disciples were in their boat and they saw Jesus coming to them walking on the water. Peter asked Jesus to call him, and so Jesus said, "Come!" But when Peter saw the wind and maybe realized the depth of water where they were, he began to sink.

We try going a little deeper, but it doesn't work. We may feel ourselves sinking even in the midst of a lesson. But, as he did with Peter, Jesus stretches out his hand and takes hold of us. It's okay. We will try to go deeper and sometimes we will fail, but we can learn if we analyze what happened or enlist the help of a more seasoned catechist to help us analyze and "fix" our effort for the next time.

We can read the Scripture again of the Lord walking on the water and imagine we are Peter. We can feel him take our hands and take hold of us. Then, when we are caught up in the Lord's embrace in our prayer, he whispers, as he did to Peter, "You of little faith, why did you doubt?" And somehow we "wanna go deeper" again.

 *For reflection/action*

BEGINNER CATECHIST
Choose one way you will go deeper in the next lesson. Line up someone who can either observe you or with whom you can debrief after the lesson to be sure you learn from the experience.

Make a calendar and keep track of the activities you use so that you remember to vary the approach. Write the names of your students too so you pay special attention to each during the course of your classes.

Make a list of all of your students and put it in a place where it will remind you to pray for each of them.

SEASONED CATECHIST
Recall your efforts to "go deeper" in a lesson when you were an inexperienced catechist. Recall one successful lesson and a

tip you can share with other catechists. Recall one lesson that was a "failure." Did you analyze that lesson? Can you share what you learned from it with the other catechists? Do it!

What are the practices that help you to continue "going deeper" in your own discipleship? Which of these practices (prayer, reading Scripture, participating in Mass, devotions, etc.) can you share with your students? Invite them to share ways they grow closer to Jesus too. You might even write something for the parish bulletin or website inviting other parishioners to try one of the ways to grow in discipleship.

Make a list of all of your students and put it in a place where it will remind you to pray for each of them.

Paddle *and* kick

When our son Nick was just a baby, I took him to "Swim and Gym for Mommy and Baby" at the local YMCA. Moms had to jump in the pool first and then the instructors would hand the babies to us. We were to begin the instruction, encouraging our tiny little ones to "paddle and kick." The babies were treading water with their little feet and joyfully splashing. On dry land, the babies seemed to still be swimming: paddling and kicking as they lay on their towels.

Moving is natural for most kids, whether they are babies, primary- and intermediate-age children, or junior high students. When we try to make them sit still for an hour or more, we may be setting ourselves up to fail. Think about where they have come from when they arrive at your class. Have they been sitting in school, or have they come from a practice for their sport team? Is your class on Saturday or Sunday? Have they just gotten up, or have they just come from Mass? Knowing where they have been just before class can help us to gauge the movement that they will need during class. Then we can provide appropriate opportunities to move and to channel their affinity for movement into productive actions.

One of the things we can do is to plan some sort of movement for every class. The United States bishops' document *National Directory for Catechesis* names six tasks, or dimensions, of catechesis (NDC pp. 61-63). Each of these tasks can be addressed using some form of movement with the students.

1. KNOWLEDGE

As catechists, we attend to teaching our students knowledge of the faith. At the end of a lesson, have students stand to answer questions. Or form two teams and have a competition. Have the teams stand on opposite sides of the room as you ask questions about the details of a Scripture story or the meanings of new faith vocabulary words.

2. LITURGY

We also have responsibility for teaching our students about the liturgy. This topic includes the Mass, the sacraments, and the liturgical year and offers many opportunities to invite movement in your class.

Young children preparing for First Communion will learn about the Mass and can practice the postures we use during the celebration. They can take turns being the "lector" who reads the Scripture story, or a part of it, to the class. Older students study the sacraments; instead of just sitting and reading they could role play each celebration. Junior high students study more about the Scriptures and can dramatize a gospel story that is in their text or perhaps act out the gospel for the coming Sunday.

Having older students visit the classes of younger children to teach them about a liturgical season is a way to get everyone moving. And nothing helps us to learn like having to teach what we have learned to someone else. My eighth-grade students would struggle with how to explain Advent to kindergarteners, so that the younger children would understand that "it isn't about Santa Claus."

Preparing our students to participate in Sunday Mass is part of our teaching about the liturgy. Focusing on the coming Sunday's season and on the Scriptures that will be proclaimed can help them to participate more fully. You might use the gospel or one of the other readings for your opening prayer. You might have young children practice the responses to the readings or the responsorial psalm. You might check with the parish music director to find out what hymns will be used on Sunday and use one of those for prayer. If some of your students play musical instruments, you could invite them to bring their instruments and play their music to accompany class prayer.

I would sometimes give my seventh graders time to work in groups and talk about what the readings have to do with the life of a seventh grader. They would then craft and deliver a "homily" to the rest of the class.

During Ordinary Time you might focus more on saints whose feasts happen on the day you have class or during the coming week. Children can then draw an image of the saint or a symbol for the saint that can be put in the prayer space. You might have students practice a particular devotion. During October, you might remind them about saying the rosary and talk about one set of mysteries in each class and say one Hail Mary. (There is not time, obviously, to say even a decade, but this "taste" can encourage them!)

Remember, these activities are not *instead of* the lesson—they *are* the lesson. Many of them can be done in ten minutes at the beginning or the end of class. Students can be asked to prepare for the activity before they come to class: to read the Sunday gospel, for example, or to ask their parents to read to them the story of the saint. If the student has done the preparation, he or she can join the group activity. If they have not prepared, they have to do the preparation while the others enjoy group work. It is not a punishment, just a natural consequence since, without the prep, they have nothing to contribute.

3. MORAL FORMATION

Moral formation is another of the tasks for which we are responsible. There may be a story in the text about someone who has to choose between good and evil. Or you might think of simple situations that call for moral decisions. Read a situation aloud and propose two possible decisions. Have students pick the decision they think is best for a follower of Jesus and to stand on the side of the room that represents that decision. Have each student explain his or her choice, and be sure to finish explaining which decision is better and why.

4. PRAYER

We are to teach prayer. We can stand and sing a hymn together, or kneel for a brief prayer. We can also take a prayer and have the children look at it line by line. Using the Prayer of Saint Francis, for example, invite children to choose a line and explain where they see injury and how they could bring pardon, where they see hatred and how they can bring love, and so on. Have each student, or partners, come to the front of the class to report on their line from the prayer. End by praying the prayer together and encouraging students to live the prayer in the ways that they reported on.

Instead of having the students stay in places for prayer, we might process to the prayer space. There are the prayers of the community that students memorize—the Our Father, the Hail Mary, the Act of Contrition, and so forth. Teach students gestures to use as they pray one of these prayers. You might even ask them to make up the gestures. Have partners each take two lines of the prayer and make up one gesture to make it efficient. Then they could teach the gestures to another class and end by praying together using the gestures.

5. COMMUNITY

Another of the six tasks of catechesis is forming disciples for community life. I made sure that my students learned to work with others—even those who were not their friends or those whom they did not particularly like. Mixing them up for group work or assigning partners sometimes rather than allowing them to choose ensured that each student would work with every other student at some point. I also frequently had the children name each other's gifts—not just talents, like being a good singer or dancer, but the gifts that can help the community. Hearing a classmate say "Regina is a good listener" or "Michael has the best ideas for our projects" or "Tory makes us all laugh and be happy" can be so affirming to a child. It can help the child to see the gifts she or he has to serve others and to strengthen the community.

One simple device I employed was a class "microphone." Some years I was able to buy a toy microphone; one time a friend had an old microphone that didn't work anymore; another time I used a paper-towel roll wrapped in aluminum foil. The idea was that no student could speak unless he or she had the microphone. They would move to retrieve the mic or to pass it to another student. It made them move, but also put an end to blurting out answers, and the students monitored that themselves: "Jerry, you don't have the mic!"

6. MISSION

The final task of catechesis is to prepare the disciples for their mission. Their mission is the mission of the church: to evangelize—to bring the good news of Jesus Christ to others through their witness and their words. Everything you do as a catechist helps to prepare them for this mission: learning about the truths of the faith, learning to pray and to participate in liturgy, learning to make decisions based on gospel values, and learning to live in community. Each of these learnings enables your students to live their faith and witness to Jesus; it also enables them to share what they believe with someone else.

Working with a partner and group work are ways they practice sharing faith with others. Perhaps, during the last few minutes of class, your children could work with a partner to decide what good news they will share at home during the week. The child practices being an evangelizer within the safety of his or her own family.

Much of the most effective evangelization comes from our witness to Jesus—the ways we live what he taught and serve those who are in need. Having opportunities to participate in service to others is an important exercise in discipleship. Rather than my simply telling the students what we would do—a food drive during Lent or a "mitten tree" in Advent—I wanted to teach them the skills they would need to live lives of service to others.

Students would be asked to identify the needs they saw in their communities. They sometimes didn't know of any and so had to ask leaders in the parish or community about them. Next they discussed what resources they had to address any of the needs. They said things like: "There are lots of elderly people in our neighborhood. We have good artists in our class who can make drawings to cheer them up." "The parish does a food drive, but sometimes the people who are hungry are lonely too. We could write notes or prayers and attach them to the canned goods so people get food and a message." "God's creation needs help on our parish grounds—there is so much litter! We can bring gloves and trash bags so it looks beautiful and inviting again."

Again, this does not have to take up a whole class; they come prepared with their ideas and then present them to the class. The class decides which service they will do.

If we don't incorporate movement sometimes, we, and our students, will start to flail about purposelessly and disrupt any learning. It's so much easier and more effective to plan for your students to "Paddle and kick!"

❋ *For reflection/action*

BEGINNER CATECHIST

Choose just one simple way to get your students moving during the next class. Use one of the ideas in this chapter or, maybe after the children have taken their seats, you can simply have them move to different seats for a change of view.

Start small when incorporating movement into your session. Let students stand up and share one thing they learned with a partner. Have them return to their own places and, if there is time, have them share what they heard.

SEASONED CATECHIST

Sometimes we stick with ways of using movement that have worked well for us. You probably have your own favorite ways to use movement. For the next class, try a new way of having your students move: for example, group work instead of partners, or acting out the Scripture instead of reading it.

Share with a fellow catechist a technique for successful "paddling and kicking" that you have used in your class. Maybe the other catechist has a new way of moving the children that you could try.

Staying afloat

I was taking a brief vacation in Cozumel, Mexico. As I was sitting by the pool reading, a scuba instructor hopped into the pool and announced that he would be giving scuba diving lessons. "What do I have to lose?" I thought. After all, it's just in a pool.

So I joined the lesson and followed the instructions about breathing and the cautions about water in my mask. When the lesson was over, the instructor invited us to join him later that day to go on a real scuba diving adventure. I was practically an expert already after that one-hour lesson, so I signed up.

We met at the front of the resort and put on our vests, masks, tanks, and all of the required gear. We were then driven in the back of a truck to the beach where we would begin our "dive," not by diving, but by simply walking into the water, going deeper and deeper. As we all got over our heads, I couldn't stay under—I just kept floating to the surface and the instructor would swim up, fetch me, adjust my vest and take me by the hand to rejoin the group. This continued to happen, three, four, five times. Each time the instructor would fix my vest and bring me back down. Finally I stayed down and enjoyed the spectacular view of underwater life.

WEIGHTS THAT GROUND US

Being held down by weights was a good thing in my dive. It "grounded" me in the midst of the water so that I could participate effectively and see the beauty that I would not have seen on the surface.

As catechists we need "grounding"—anchoring—too. That grounding is our own discipleship to Jesus Christ, our love of God and the church, and our knowledge of the faith and the life of prayer. In the depths of our hearts we know the beauty of the Catholic faith.

We share that grounding with our students when we help them to see the beauty of the faith and help them to delve deeper into it each year.

Another way to ground them in the faith is to incorporate the arts, both performing arts and fine arts. Bring in an illustration of a Scripture story and ask what they notice. Think of a hymn that relates to the lesson and have them pick out the words that comfort or challenge them. Sing the hymn or, if your class doesn't sing, listen to a recording of the hymn.

I am sure you have heard the saying, "You are what you eat." Feed them with beauty, with religious paintings of our tradition, with poetry that relates to the content of the lesson. Use Robert Frost's "The Road Not Taken" when you are discussing moral decisions, or the children's book *It's Not Easy Being Green,* by Kermit the Frog, to talk about the dignity of each person.

As a junior high catechist, I was having difficulty getting my class to discuss a topic. Then I attended an in-service at which the adult participants had trouble discussing what the speaker asked us to discuss. I realized that not everyone is ready to jump in and discuss without some time to think. I started to have discussions that began with the students taking time to think about the question first, or to draw their idea or write about it. Then we took time for them to share their thoughts with just one friend. (I saw at the adult gathering that no one went to share with a stranger. Why should we make students do that? We say friends are a gift from God, but we seldom let them work together.) Then the two friends would join with two other friends and combine their ideas. The group would then present their ideas to the whole class so we could continue discussing. Finally, we would talk about how what we heard changed our thinking and what we might do about it.

WEIGHTS THAT SINK US

When the dive in Cozumel was over, the instructor led us back to the shallow water of the coast. When I reached the shallow water, I tried to stand and to my horror, I could not get up. Certain I had been bitten by some sea creature whose bite had paralyzed me, I screamed, "Help, I can't move!" The instructor came running and calmly said, "Carole, take the weights out of your vest." Sure enough, my pockets were filled with heavy weights—which had been placed there by the instructor each time he swam up to retrieve me. Once I removed the weights I carried, I could stand. I could walk again! And I could float without sinking.

Once in awhile, our inability to be successful is due not to any outside influence but to the weights we carry around in our own pockets. That is why it is so vital to analyze each lesson we teach, how it went, and how engaged the students were or were not. The classes that do not go well may be the result of the weights we carry.

One "weight" that may keep us down is that we are not comfortable with Scripture and therefore don't use the word of God effectively with our class. Catechists need not be Scripture scholars, though we certainly should know Scripture and be growing toward a greater understanding. There are easy ways to bring more Scripture into our lessons. We might simply share one of our favorite Scripture stories and why it is our favorite. Maybe each student could share a favorite each subsequent week.

Take a Scripture quote from the current lesson and write it on the board or on a large piece of paper as the "quote of the day." Have the children talk about what the quote means and how we can live its message. Use this as a way to begin class or to begin prayer. Borrow resources that your parish lectors use to help them understand and prepare to proclaim the Sunday readings. There are online resources too that you might access. Share the insights you gain from these resources with your class in an age-appropriate way.

Invite children to close their eyes and imagine they are one of the characters in a Scripture story: Zacchaeus in the tree, the older son in the prodigal son story, one of the lepers who was cleansed. Have them share how they felt, what they would do next.

Perhaps it is not being comfortable with praying together that is the weight in your pocket. Have a notebook or poster where children can write their prayer intentions. Or focus the prayer by praying a brief line that each child can complete. "I thank you, God, for..." or "Lord, I ask you for your help for..."

You can use photos—from magazines or ones you print from websites—to help children compose prayers and develop compassion. Have them study the photos and think about what the person in the photo might pray for. Ask what the person in the photo might need and then have them compose a prayer asking God for what they think the person might need.

Do a "go-around" to begin prayer. Ask each student just to say a sentence about something that is on her or his mind as you begin class: "I am worried about the math test I will have tomorrow." Then go around again and have each student pray about the thing that they named in the first go-around: "Holy Spirit, inspire me to study the right things tonight."

Your own comfort with prayer will help the students grow in their ability to pray.

One of the issues that catechists often name as a weight sinking them is trying to do group work. I tried having students work in groups several times only to have it be a disaster. Finally I really analyzed what had happened, and I learned a lot about what I could do to ensure a positive experience of group work. First, be sure the task is crystal clear. Part of the failure in my group-work classes was that they weren't sure what they were supposed to do in their group. So time was spent as they tried to figure out the task or asked me questions, which meant the other groups were unsupervised. Be sure the task is clear to every group: "Choose one of the gifts of the Holy Spirit and name someone you see using that gift and how that person uses it."

A second mistake I made was not giving a time limit. The time should be adequate for the task, but no longer. Groups who were thinking they had the rest of the class time to do their task were understandably not in any hurry to complete their work. "You will have ten minutes to do your work." Then be sure to stick to the time allotted.

The next mistake I made was not holding them accountable for the "product" of their group work. There has to be an assignment given to them at the start of the group work. If students just sat in their groups and talked, they were tempted to wander off the topic. If they know that the group will have to make a report to the class at the end of the ten minutes, they are likely to stay on task.

Three steps to good group work: clear task, clear time frame which is adequate—neither too long or too short, and accountability for a "product" of their labors. Now, weights removed, you can stay afloat!

The weights in my pockets made it impossible for me to stand let alone to float. The problem many of us often have when things go wrong is that we look for someone else to blame: "My class is so unruly! I can't ever do group work with them because they are too disruptive." "They just won't discuss anything as much as I ask. They just aren't interested. Or maybe they are just not very bright." We fail to notice the weights in our pockets that cause us to fail, and with us, our children too.

Whenever we are in the waters of catechesis, we have to watch out for pirates too. Pirates can steal our joy in sharing the faith, and our joy in the children who have been entrusted to us. Pirates put weights in our pockets and distract us from looking there, so we become discouraged and think we just aren't cut out to be catechists. They feed us with words of negativity and cynicism. Don't let the pirates get to you!

As I walked the beach this morning, there was a teenager with a small surf board who went running into the gulf. He ran, threw the board into the waves, and hopped on. He immediately fell off, face-first into the water. As I came by he was declaring "Ouch" and grabbing his knee. But he got right up and smiled at me, saying, "It will take some time." And I am certain that whatever time it takes for him to ride the waves, he will consider being able to surf worth it.

You have been called by God and the church to teach the children in your class about Jesus and how to live a happy life now and forever. It is so worthwhile. It will take some time, but, with grace, you can stay afloat.

 *For reflection/action*

BEGINNER CATECHIST

Think about the weights you carry in your own pockets that sink you. What part of the lessons are you uncomfortable doing? Ask a seasoned catechist to help you get rid of the weights by suggesting ways to be more comfortable with the parts of the lesson or the topics you are less comfortable teaching.

Next class session, try group work for just a small, manageable task. Remember, clear task, clear time frame and accountability. Analyze how it went. What can you do to make it even better next time?

Try not to complain about your students but to reflect on what you can do differently to direct their energy and enthusiasm.

SEASONED CATECHIST

Identify the weights that ground you as a catechist. What is your strength? How can you share that strength with other catechists?

Sometimes even seasoned catechists can be unknowingly carrying weights around that sink them. Is there still part of the lesson you avoid? Or a teaching technique you have never tried? Why? Who can assist you in addressing and overcoming your discomfort?

Remember that sometimes your students have weights in their pockets that sink them too. Like me on my scuba dive, sometimes the weights were put there by others—a friend's rejection, parents' separation, etc. When they are struggling, help them to identify the weights and suggest ways they can, with God's grace, cope with the weights or get rid of them if they can.

Try not to complain about your students but to reflect on what you can do differently to direct their energy and enthusiasm.

Life savers

In 1912, candymaker Clarence Crane decided to supplement his line of chocolate candies with a "summer" candy that would not melt. The circular candies with the hole in the middle were called Life Savers® since they looked like miniature life preservers.

As I walk the beach, I see children using flotation devices in the same colors as the basic Life Savers candies: red, green, yellow, orange, and off-white. These lightweight plastic tubes would not stand up well in the rougher, deeper waters that would surround shipwrecked passengers. But here near the shore they are a perfect way to ride the waves and enjoy the water.

Life Savers' original slogan was, "For that stormy breath." Life Savers were problem solvers: they would freshen our breath and save the day!

But what can save us when our class session is a disaster? An ounce of prevention, the old saying goes, is worth a pound of cure. As the pack of fruit-flavored Life Savers had five flavors, let's consider five "life savers" to prevent or to salvage a class-gone-badly.

FIVE LESSON-SAVERS

1. Preparation. There is no substitute for preparing the session well with attention to my unique students and their abilities. We begin to know their preferences for engaging with the content, and, though we may not name these as such, we become aware of the "multiple intelligences." These are ways of learning, and students differ in their preferred ways. Varying our lessons and the activities can ensure we engage the students and meet their different ways of learning. Sometimes we discuss a lesson; other times we can do a time line. We invite students to organize information about the books of the Bible, or we have them make a cross during Lent or compose a new hymn to honor Mary. We have them work cooperatively sometimes and reflect alone other times. Each student's learning style is addressed in some way during the course of our classes.

Sometimes, I admit, I did not prepare for my class. Whatever my excuse, I would go to class and merely "fake it." On occasion it went all right—usually when it was a topic with which I was very familiar, or when there was a question or activity in the book that just happened to interest the students. Mostly though, if I didn't prepare, I paid the price by having a bad experience—and the students paid too. Even if we take just fifteen minutes to prepare, it can make all the difference. The first "life saver" is preparation for the lesson.

2. Changing direction. There were also times when I *did* prepare, but I could feel the class taking a turn for the worse. Sometimes, we just have to change direction in the midst of the lesson to vary the activities. Maybe we have been doing group work, and in their enthusiasm, students are getting too loud and unruly. Have them stop the group work, return to their places, and think about how they would summarize their discussion. After some quiet time, have each student share her or his summary. Maybe you sense boredom as students read the chapter, or pehaps they have no response when you ask a question at the end. Have them join a partner and rewrite a section of the chapter to tell the content to a younger child. Do the students seem sleepy? Have them stand, reach for the sky, reach for the floor, then sit in a new place. Do the students seem agitated? Maybe they just came from having a test or losing a game? Then play some quiet music and ask about their favorite prayers. The second life saver is varying the activity to counter potential problems.

3. Plan B. Another trick I learned came when the children did not do what the guide said they would do. Maybe it was that discussion that the guide said would enthrall them for twenty minutes but was actually over in sixty seconds; maybe it was the activity that the guide said would consume fifteen minutes but your students finished in five. Maybe you chose the wrong option and found your students were not interested in or not capable of doing the one you chose. From these experiences — and I had them all! — I learned to always have a Plan B.

I always brought something "extra" that could be used on these occasions. I would have a copy of a page of quotations for each child. These might be Scripture quotes or other quotes related to the main topic of their texts, like prayer or church. I would distribute these and have each student choose the quote that she or he found either comforting or challenging. I might ask them to share the quote, or to print and decorate the quote. I might have copies of a drawing of a labyrinth and have them use their index finger to "walk" the labyrinth while I played soft music. For younger children, I would have index cards with one of our faith words printed on each card. Either alone or with a partner, the children would make up a sentence using the faith word. Or each card could have the name of one of the biblical people we had learned about, and the task would be to retell the story of the person on their card. Whenever I had to use one of my Plan Bs, I would make up a new one. The third life saver is to always have at least one Plan B up your sleeve!

4. Look back. The first three life savers have to do with planning ahead. But another life saver is looking back to look ahead. In his book *First You Have to Row a Little Boat*, author Richard Bode tells the story of learning to sail. First, he goes in a rowboat and there reflects on the fact that the row boat is one of the few forms of transportation in which you do not face the direction in which you are traveling. When you row a boat, you focus on where you have been and that tells you if you are on course or not. There is a T-shirt that says, "I've learned so much from my mistakes, I think I'll make a few more." We can learn from both our mistakes and from our successes.

Look at the shore of the last lesson. Close your eyes and see the children. What were they doing? Do you see the expressions on their faces? What are the signs of learning that you see? What are the signs of joy in that class? Look back and see if you are headed in the right direction to form these young disciples. Let this reflection inform your planning for the next class session. Having someone observe your class and offer feedback is another way of looking back. I remember reading a quote from Franklin P. Jones that said, "Honest criticism is hard to take, particularly from a relative, a friend, an acquaintance, or a stranger." No one ever said it would be easy, but looking back to look ahead is the fourth life saver.

5. Hope. The Merriam-Webster Dictionary defines hope as "to cherish a desire with anticipation; to expect with confidence." You said yes to becoming a catechist, reluctantly or enthusiastically, because you hoped. You hoped you could learn to be a good one; you hoped you would make a difference in your students' lives; you hoped you would be able to form disciples who would know and live their faith. Saint Clement of Alexandria said, "If you do not hope, you will not find what is beyond your hopes."

My hopes as a beginning catechist were very simple and very practical: I hoped I could survive a lesson and I hoped no one would get hurt. I know I set the bar very low, but if I could achieve those two things, I could continue.

I read an advertisement a few years ago that I have never forgotten. It read, "Take people from church membership to discipleship in 3 hours." If that had been my hope, I would have been sorely disappointed, and I am sure I would have quit after two lessons when the three hours would have been up!

Technological advances seem to have made us a more impatient people. When I log on the internet and ask a question, I want an immediate answer. Forming disciples—young or old—takes time. Having that perspective on our ministry is critical.

In the First Letter of Peter, he writes that the followers of Jesus should always be ready to "give an account for the hope that is in you" (1 Peter 3:15). What is your reason for hope? What is your hope as a catechist? What do you hope for the children entrusted to you?

The Letter to the Hebrews refers to hope as an "anchor of the soul...sure and steadfast" (Hebrews 6:19). The *Catechism of the Catholic Church* says we are "buoyed up by hope" (#1818). The Czech poet Vaclav Havel wrote: "Hope is an orientation of the spirit, an orientation of the heart. It is not the conviction that something will turn out well, but the certainty that something makes sense, regardless of how it turns out."

We know hope, not only as anchor and buoy and orientation of the heart, but as a theological virtue that offers a perspective to all of life. Hope sees all in the light of eternity, trusting in Christ's promises and the grace of the Holy Spirit. Hope is big; it sees beyond this one class that didn't go well.

The symbol for hope is the anchor, which, in its more traditional form, looks a lot like a cross. Just because you offered to be a catechist does not preclude the necessity of your bearing a cross or two. We can't swim on the beach; hope, our anchor and buoy, can't be found in the cabana—we have to risk entering the water.

Singer Leonard Cohen's song "Anthem" has a great message of hope. He reminds us that whatever we do, it will never be perfect; everything has a crack in it. "That's how the light gets in."

I used to think that when there was a "crack" in something—a relationship or a project or a lesson—it was broken and worthless. Cohen's song made me look at cracked things differently. The brokenness was a clue to what was needed to make it better or stronger. I just had to pay attention to the light. When a lesson "breaks," if we look carefully, we can see the light trying to get through to us. That light—not blaming or, worse, quitting—is what will bring hope and help us to fix the next lesson. Sometimes we can't see and identify the light that is coming through, so we ask the DRE or another catechist to help us. And sometimes we help them when their effort has a crack. Hope is the fifth life saver, or maybe the first, really.

One time when Jesus and his disciples were in a boat, a storm arose. Jesus was sleeping though the storm but the disciples were so afraid they woke him and begged, "Save us, Lord; we are perishing!" (Do you feel like you are perishing sometimes during a class?) Jesus calmed the storm. "What sort of man is this," they mused, "whom even the winds and the sea obey?" (Matthew 8:23-27). Do you imagine his grace can't help you calm a group of students?

Life Savers had a commercial at one time that proclaimed, "Life Savers, a part of living." Life savers are a part of catechizing too. Look for them, use them, and taste the hope they offer.

 *For reflection/action*

BEGINNER CATECHIST

Set aside time for planning the lesson ahead of time. Try to find a specific time each week that would work for you—Friday night after dinner or Tuesday right after work. Make a plan for evaluating each lesson after class. Pay attention to what you can learn from both failures and successes. Keep a notebook or smartphone handy to jot notes immediately after class so you can keep those in mind for the next class.

Work on a Plan B to keep in your bookbag.

Write one hope you have for your students. Keep it in your guide where you will see it before each class, and it will keep your eyes on the big picture.

SEASONED CATECHIST

Think about the life savers who helped you to be a better catechist. Thank one of them with an e-mail, text message, phone call, or a prayer.

Sometimes we can get too comfortable as experienced catechists. Focus on planning a new approach to your next lesson. Evaluate how the lesson went. Were there any "cracks"? Did you see the light?

Write one hope you have for your students. Keep it in your guide where you will see it before each class, and it will keep your eyes on the big picture.

Life preservers

According to Merriam-Webster, a life preserver is "a device designed to save a person from drowning." Unlike the lightweight blow-up toys that children play with in the water, life preservers are life-saving even in deep waters and rough seas— like the waters we sometimes find ourselves in when we are catechists.

Unlike the Life Saver candy, with more than two grams of carbohydrate and more than two grams of sugar in each one, the life preservers a catechist needs have to be nourishing. We need to be strong in mind and body and spirit—strong in faith—to be able to teach others about Jesus.

The *National Catechetical Directory* describes what characteristics the spiritual life of a catechist should have (NDC pp. 228-230). Each of these is a life preserver.

TEN LIFE PRESERVERS FOR THE CATECHIST

The first characteristic *is love of the Trinitarian God.* How do we grow in love of the Father, Son, and Holy Spirit? The same way we grow in love of a friend or a spouse: by getting to know them better and by experiencing their presence. How are you growing in knowledge and love of God? What might help you?

The second characteristic is *love of the church*, love of the pope, and love of all God's people. Again, learning about the church throughout her history—the good and the bad parts—can help us to appreciate the church and love all that the church has done to educate people, to uphold human rights, to care for the ill and dying, and to stand up for those who are oppressed.

Third, we, as catechists, are called especially to witness through our lives to what we teach. We are to *practice our faith and give evidence of the virtues* of faith and love and hope, as well as courage in living our faith and joy in our discipleship. Living these virtues takes discipline and effort, but they will help to preserve our lives as catechists.

Fourth, catechists need the life preserver of *prayer*. No amount of preparation can make us effective without our grounding in conversation with God. Praying for our students can put us in tune with their needs, and listening to the Spirit can enable us to respond to their needs to learn the faith in ways that suit their age and stage of development.

Fifth, since catechesis is a part of the evangelizing mission of the church, we have chosen to engage in this mission and have to develop a dedication that will see us through whatever storms might jar and scare us. This *dedication to the mission*, along with a love for our students, will ensure our zeal for proclaiming the Good News.

Sixth, our own *participation in our parish community and in the Eucharist* is essential, both because the community will support us and because we then will witness to the importance of the community of faith to our lives as disciples of Jesus. Our participation in Sunday Mass is especially critical. There we find life preservers in the word of God, in the sacrament of the Eucharist, and in the living community. Availing ourselves of these sources of nourishment is life preserving.

Seventh, the spiritual life of the catechist is also character-ized by *devotion to Mary*, the mother who catechized Jesus. Likewise, we may find nourishment in the devotion to our patron saints or patrons of catechists.

Eighth, I once read that it takes 200 hours of training to become a dealer at a casino in Indiana. How much time am I willing to spend to become a catechist? To become a better catechist? *Learning is a life preserver.* Your parish or your dio-cese might offer courses to help you grow; there are courses or webinars offered by Catholic universities, colleges, and associations and companies. There are wonderful books on theology, Scripture, sacraments, etc., that are available in print or as e-books. What area do you need to know more about? Your pastor or DRE or principal might be able to suggest a good book, or a seasoned catechist might share a book that helped her or him.

Certainly, *knowing more about Scripture* will be a life preserv-er for us. The Letter of Paul to the Romans says, "For whatever was written in earlier times was written for our instruction, so that through perseverance and the encouragement of the Scriptures we might have hope." Can you place a Bible beside your bed, or next to the chair you relax in? Perhaps each morn-ing, or before bed, you could read just a few lines of Scripture to think about for the next twenty-four hours. Maybe while you are on the treadmill at the gym you could play a Scripture passage on your iPod.

Author Barbara Brown Taylor writes in *The Preaching Life* about what is required to proclaim the Good News: "engaging in the discipline of reading and studying and arguing with and meditating on and living with the word of God in Scripture. I mean letting its stories come to life so that they become daily points of reference and sources of increasing insight." Then we can talk easily about God changing people's plans as he changed Mary's or people being faithful to God even in suffering, as Job was, or good disciples always pointing beyond themselves to Jesus, as his cousin John did.

One of the areas we need to constantly keep up with is technology. No matter what age we are or what our experience has been—or has not been—with technology, every week there is something new. There are two reasons for us to keep up with developments: one is to make use of technology for catechesis. The other reason to keep up with the latest in technological breakthroughs is to be able to give examples and make references that connect to the students' real lives.

The uses of technology in the catechetical session are myriad. There are the older technologies to employ such as DVDs and CDs. Using a DVD to present a topic or a CD to enhance prayer are still excellent ways to vary the class experience. You might have a computer and projector that will project the lesson so it can be done together. Smartboard activities are a good way to engage the whole class while having individuals involved in the game or quiz too. You might skype with a guest speaker who is an expert in the topic you are studying. By the time this book is published, there will be new uses and gadgets that we haven't dreamed of yet! Students might bring their own portable internet devices and, with supervision, go on the Vatican website (*www.vatican.va*) or the United States bishops' website (*www.USCCB.org*) to find the latest papal document or church news. It can be fun to film students doing a role play or to have them interview people on a chapter topic, recording their interviews so they can share them with the class.

Technology can also help you as a catechist with communication and information. Always check with your director for any policies that pertain to using technology with students or families. If parish policies allow, you might use it to keep in touch with students who are ill, send assignments home, send positive notes to parents and guardians, or announce a performance or service opportunity.

Technology is also a life preserver for you. Use it for researching a topic, or to find a Scripture passage to use in your class. You can use technology to attend a webinar, to engage in a conference call with other catechists to share ideas, or to check out resources for you and your class. You can also look for the answers to questions your class might ask, being sure to vet the site or checking with your pastor or leader for a recommendation. There are national organizations and some Catholic higher education institutions that offer discussion or question and answer sites where you will find what catechists or other ministers are discussing.

Poet Allen Ginsberg wrote, "Whoever controls the media, the images, controls the culture." If we are to influence our cultures with the gospel message, we have to, perhaps not control, but certainly use the media of our time.

The ninth important life preserver for catechists is *imagination*. Jesus certainly had imagination when he looked at the twelve men he had chosen. In spite of their failure to understand and their seeking places next to him and their running away when he was arrested, Jesus saw in them the leaders of his followers. He saw that, with the Holy Spirit's coming, they would be able to proclaim and to lead, to convert and to build local communities. We have to be able to imagine who our children can become; we have to believe in them and see the best in them. Was it not Jesus' belief in his apostles that enabled them to rise to the occasion?

In the Book of Numbers in the Bible, we read the story of

Balaam the prophet and how his donkey saw the angel of the Lord and listened when Balaam neither heard nor listened. That's why the tenth life preserver we're considering here is *listening*, even when the message comes from unlikely places. Sometimes we set out and are determined to go *our* way. Listen; watch; maybe the signs are God's way of trying something else. Maybe we are discouraged as a primary children's catechist and someone says, "Maybe you'd be better with junior high kids." We need to listen, to be open to change and suggestions. Sometimes there's an angel of the Lord redirecting us! We listen to our bodies too, and respond when we need rest or time alone or a break.

THIRSTING FOR GOD

The message of Jesus is counter-cultural. If we reflect on the forms that water can take, we can consider how each may be seen in our contemporary culture and how the gospel would have us see it.

Water can be ice, that which freezes out those not like us. The disciple sees ice as that which might ease pain, or that which protects the life living beneath it. Water can be steam, and our culture values a fine sauna and accepts the steam of sweat shops that produce cheaper goods for consumption. The disciple sees steam as the warmth of inclusion, that which can remove the wrinkles of worry or promote healing.

H_2O in its liquid form may be valued by our culture as power to be harnessed, a resource to be consumed. The disciple sees water as a precious gift to be enjoyed and shared. The disciple is concerned about fresh water for all people and about preserving it to sustain and refresh future generations. When water turns into fog, it is another story. Tiny droplets of water come together to form a ground-level cloud that can leave us disoriented and without a clear path to follow. It is a reminder of the mystery of faith.

Some folks say we humans are attracted to water because we are more than 60% water ourselves. We sweat—our culture says that's okay as long as we do it for money. Disciples know that sweating is good as long as we are spreading the reign of God. We cry, and many in our culture shed tears for their possessions; disciples weep over injustice, oppression, alienation. Our life preserver may be simply reflecting on the ways we see the waters of our lives.

Jesus calls to us across the ages, saying, as he said to the Samaritan woman at the well, "Give me a drink." And he speaks this request in the voices of the children who sit before us, saying, though not aloud, "I am thirsty for God's Word. I am thirsty to know I am loved and valued."

And then, we hear Jesus' reassurance, "Whoever drinks of the water I shall give will never thirst" (John 4:14). And we know, as his catechists, we'll never be thirsty.

 *For reflection/action*

BEGINNER CATECHIST
Which of the life preservers mentioned in this chapter have worked for you? Is there one of the life preservers you have not tried but will try during the coming week?

Think about each of your students and what you imagine them doing to serve others and to grow in their faith. Pray for each of them.

SEASONED CATECHIST

What other life preserver have you used to help you as a catechist? Share your life preserver with your catechist group.

What learning have you done lately about your faith? Review what you have learned. Plan a way to share that learning with your students.

Now dive!

It was an astounding sight! I had just arrived at the beach for my walk when I saw it: A very small child far out in the deep water, bobbing happily in the midst of gentle though high waves. "How can it be?" I asked myself, searching the shore for someone who was watching this tiny child, and simultaneously preparing to run into the water myself. Then—could it be—the child seemed to rise above the water! Yes, the child stood now above the water because his father, on whose shoulders the youngster was riding, had stood up and was no longer submerged.

The deep waters of teaching the faith need not frighten us when we ride on the shoulders of those who have navigated these waters before us. We have learned, and can continue to learn, by reflecting on the experiences of being catechized. What worked with us? What were the memorable lessons you had as a child or as a youth? We can even think about lessons we have learned as adults and why we found them engaging—or not.

We are carried on the shoulders of catechists throughout the ages, whose joy and struggle have also been to teach other disciples. We stand on the shoulders of catechists like Saint

Augustine, who having experienced conversion in his own life, was then eager to bring others to Christ. Augustine wrote to the catechist Deogratias in *Catechizing of the Uninstructed* (*De Catechizandis Rudibus*): "The very fact that persons who require to be instructed in the faith are brought so frequently to you, ought to help you to understand that your discourse is not displeasing to others as it is displeasing to yourself; and you ought not to consider yourself unfruitful, simply because you do not succeed in setting forth in such a manner as you desire the things which you discern" (#4). The saint reminds us that lessons we judge as failure may, in fact, have touched those we catechize. We are, after all, instruments of God's work, and his grace enables us — beyond our own abilities — to teach his word.

We are carried on the shoulders of Saint Charles Borromeo, patron of catechists, who reminds us, "If we wish to make progress in the service of God we must begin every day of our life with new eagerness. We must keep ourselves in the presence of God as much as possible and have no other view or end in all our actions but the divine honor."

Saint Andrew Kim Taegon, Saint Paul Chong Hasang, and the Korean martyrs, whose feast we celebrate on September 20, were catechists martyred for spreading the faith in Korea. In his final exhortation, Saint Andrew Kim said, "I urge you to remain steadfast in faith, so that at least we will all reach heaven and there rejoice together."

We are carried on the shoulders of all of our ancestors in faith and by the whole communion of saints, so we can go deeper into the waters. We are carried by Jesus too, who whispers as we begin each class, "Be not afraid!"

The hymn *Agua de Vida, Water of Life* by Jaime Cortez has the beautiful line in its refrain, "Water of life, holy reminder, touching, renewing the body of Christ." The waters of baptism renew us as they bring us to new life in Christ. Other waters can renew us too in less profound but also important ways.

Some people go to the water to work. They fish or test the waters for research, or they are instructors for water sports, or they are captains, crew, or tour guides on boats. Many other people go to the water to play. They swim, they boat, they surf, they float, they ski or tube—they are refreshed. Those for whom the water is their work often say that their love of the water makes working on and in it refreshing too. Holy water is used to bless, and it is used to refresh our baptismal promises.

Jesus must have been refreshed by water. He was drawn to the Jordan for baptism and he went to the sea to call his first followers. He must have loved the Sea of Galilee, for he so often went there and boated with the disciples. It was the Sea of Galilee that he walked on and where the disciples had the miraculous catch of fish when they followed Jesus' direction. Even as they still were fishermen catching fish, as they rode the waters he was teaching them to be catchers of people. Was Jesus walking along the shore when this image came to him? "The kingdom of heaven is like a net thrown into the sea, which collects fish of every kind" (Matthew 13:47).

For catechists, there is a time for staying in shallow water and a time to go deeper. When we are new at this catechizing enterprise, we can stick close to shore as we test the waters and check for any unseen currents that can drag us away from our goal. But to stay always in the shallow water will eventually bore us, and then we will be boring to our students. In fact, the students may, on their own, venture deeper and swim away from us perhaps.

Russian Olympic gold medal swimmer Alexander Popov said, "The water is your friend...you don't have to fight with water, just share the same spirit as the water, and it will help you move." Being a catechist means sharing the same Spirit who moved the waters of creation and who appeared as a dove over the waters of the Jordan and whom we call upon to bless the waters of baptism. In the *General Directory for Catechesis* we read, "Neither catechesis nor evangelization is possible without the action of God working through his Spirit. In catechetical praxis, neither the most advanced pedagogical techniques nor the most talented catechist can ever replace the silent and unseen action of the Holy Spirit" (#288). If we are faithful catechists, we do not swim alone. And the Holy Spirit will never let us sink and drown.

For twelve years I lived in lower Manhattan, New York, just a block from the Hudson River. To reach my parish, St. Joseph Chapel of St. Peter Parish, on Sundays, I would walk along the river. There was a beautiful view of the Statue of Liberty as I walked back to my condo. You know her message, I am sure: "Give me your tired, your poor, your huddled masses yearning to breathe free..." As I stared at the statue and recalled the words of the Emma Lazarus poem, it always brought to mind the words of Jesus: "Come to me, all who are weary and heavy-laden, and I will give you rest" (Matthew 11:28).

Both the statue and the words of Jesus reminded me of catechists. You, like Lady Liberty, stand beside the door, offering welcome to all. Young people too are sometimes weary from their studies and their chores; they are sometimes heavily laden with worry over a parent's job loss or a sibling's illness or their failures in school. Children who live in poverty—whether material or spiritual—yearn to breathe free. You lift, not the lamp that Lady Liberty raises, but the light of Christ to guide and warm their way.

And Jesus said to the disciples who tried to keep the children away for him, "Let the children come to me and do not prevent them" (Luke 18:16). You, catechist, stand at the door to be certain the children find their way closer to Jesus. And then, Jesus adds, "the kingdom of God belongs to such as these," these children. Remember too that Jesus also told his followers that unless they would "become like children, you will not enter the kingdom of heaven" (Matthew 18:3).

Children love to come to the water. They may be hesitant at first, as we all are, to jump in, and so they take it more slowly sometimes. I watch them: a child sticks a toe in the water or a hand, screams with delight, runs away from the water, turns and looks back, runs back to the water, and puts more of himself in—a whole foot or two hands.

Like children, a new catechist may explore the water of catechesis a bit gingerly—approaching, testing, running away, coming back, going deeper. You have succeeded and failed, you have laughed and cried. You have lived the works of mercy as you visited the ill and instructed the students, as you prayed, and as you both comforted those who grieved and forgave the troublemakers. You saw those who were hungry or thirsty and saw to it that their needs were met. In the eyes of those little ones (and even older ones, though they would not admit it) to whom you proclaimed God's love and showed God's love, you *do* walk on water.

When I was on a pilgrimage on Our Lady's Island in Wexford, Ireland, I was told the customary way of walking around the island is with one foot on the land and one foot in the lake. This, our guide, explained was to remind us we have one foot on earth and the other in heaven. What I learned from walking this way was that I need to hang on to my fellow pilgrims. And so, as catechists, we do too. Hang on!

Years ago I read an article about how we all need a coach in life—someone who will help us train, encourage us to do our best, bring us refreshment after our exertion, celebrate our wins with us, and bemoan our losses while still getting us to begin again. We need catechetical coaches who will work with us like this. Get a coach!

One of the most dire responsibilities we have as catechists is to make sure the mission continues. During our first year it may seem too overwhelming to even think about who will come after us—but once we have that first year completed, or nearly completed, it is time to mentor a future catechist. There is someone you know, maybe someone who volunteers in another role in your program, who has the qualities a good catechist needs. Mentor someone!

When Jesus and Mary celebrated with their friends at the wedding in Cana, things could have gone badly for the host if the guests had discovered all the wine had been consumed. But Mary bought the need to Jesus, Jesus responded to their need, and the water was made into wine. Do you have any doubt that the Lord, the Christ, God's Son, can turn the wateriest lessons into the finest wine of learning?

So, catechist, you may have begun your ministry asking, "Why me?" And now you may be saying, "Why me *again*?" The answer is because the Lord needs you and the church needs you, and because there are ways you will speak the message of Jesus to the children in a way that no one else in their lives can do. Now dive in, catechist!

 *For reflection/action*

BEGINNER CATECHIST

Whom will you mentor? How will you begin?

Invite one student for each class session who will stand at the door with you and welcome the other students.

SEASONED CATECHIST:

List the works of mercy on a poster and hang it in your class. When a class session is over, have students choose one of the works to do as their mission during the week.

Identify people in the parish who are recent immigrants who would be willing to share their story. They can be asked to share the difficulties they encountered and the importance of the welcomes they received.

My Story, Part II

The _____ Catechist

Now that the last lesson is over, I want to shout _____!
If I had to sum up this year's experiences in two words, the
words would be _____ and _____.

The children I taught started out _____ and now
they are _____. Our most memorable class experience was when we _____. And I will never forget the time that one of the students, _____, said
_____.

I have grown in my own faith as I _____. One
important thing I learned about being a catechist is that I
can always _____. And I am grateful to God for
_____.

There were always people to help me, especially _____, who showed me how to
_____. I had some good ideas too and I
shared a way to _____ with _____.

My hope for the students who "swam" with me is that they have
_____ and never _____. As I
look to the next year as a catechist I feel _____
and I know that I can _____.

My story may not end with "happily ever after" right now, but
it continues as I hold on to _____.